SCIENCE IN
KING TUT'S
TOMB

by Tammy Enz

CAPSTONE PRESS
a capstone imprint

Capstone Captivate is published by Capstone Press, an imprint of Capstone.
1710 Roe Crest Drive
North Mankato, Minnesota 56003
www.capstonepub.com

Library of Congress Cataloging-in-Publication Data
Names: Enz, Tammy, author.
Title: Science in King Tut's tomb / by Tammy Enz.
Description: North Mankato, Minnesota : Capstone Press, an imprint of Capstone, [2021] | Series: The science of history | Includes bibliographical references and index. | Audience: Ages: 8-11 | Audience: Grades: 4-6 | Summary: "One of the most well-known pharaohs from ancient Egypt was King Tut. Did you know that science played a big role in ancient Egypt? Find out how the Egyptian pyramids were engineered. Learn about the science behind King Tut's mummy. And discover how modern technology helps us learn more about King Tut's life and death"-- Provided by publisher. Identifiers: LCCN 2021002766 (print) | LCCN 2021002767 (ebook) | ISBN 9781496695758 (hardcover) | ISBN 9781496696939 (paperback) | ISBN 9781977159144 (pdf) | ISBN 9781977159212 (kindle edition) Subjects: LCSH: Tutankhamen, King of Egypt--Tomb--Juvenile literature. | Pyramids--Egypt--Juvenile literature. | Technology--Egypt--History--Juvenile literature.
Classification: LCC DT87.5 .E59 2021 (print) | LCC DT87.5 (ebook) | DDC 932/.014092--dc23
LC record available at https://lccn.loc.gov/2021002766
LC ebook record available at https://lccn.loc.gov/2021002767

Editorial Credits
Editors, Angie Kaelberer and Aaron Sautter; Designer, Kazuko Collins; Media Researcher, Svetlana Zhurkin; Production Specialist, Kathy McColley

Image Credits
Alamy: Jeff Morgan 03, 11; Associated Press: Saedi Press, 19; Bridgeman Images: © Look and Learn, 5, Look and Learn/Peter Jackson Collection, 17; Dreamstime: Edwardgerges, 32, Photoguns, 25, Sergio Bertino, 31; Getty Images: AFP/Mohamed El-Shahed, 39, ClassicStock/Sipley, 7; Library of Congress: 10, 15; Newscom: akg-images/André Held, 37, Album, 24, Heritage Images/Historica Graphica Collection, 43, MCT/Boswell, 12, robertharding Productions, 26, World History Archive, 34; Shutterstock: Alexander Tolstykh, 41 (bottom), Billion Photos, cover (top), Digital Images Studio, 21, El Greco 1973, cover (bottom), 1 (top), Emir Kaan, 33, Everett Collection, 13, 23, Jaroslav Moravcik, 29, KamimiArt (design element), 1 (bottom) and throughout, Kore, 44, Maxal Tamor, 8, mountainpix, 42, Nick Brundle, 41 (top), Omer Bugra, 35, Orhan Cam, 45, Peter Hermes Furian, 9, vchal, 20, Vladimir Wrangel, 38, Yuriy Buyvol, 27

TABLE OF CONTENTS

Words in **bold** text are included in the glossary.

CHAPTER 1

TOMBS AND TREASURE

If you were an Egyptian pharaoh almost 5,000 years ago, you were considered more than a king. Pharaohs were thought to be part human and part god. How they were buried was very important. Their tombs housed everything the ancient Egyptians believed pharaohs needed to journey into the next life.

Many pharaohs spent years planning their burials. They built huge tombs filled with jewels and gold. Over the years, most of these tombs were looted. Their treasures were stolen. Much of the history of early Egypt disappeared along with the treasure. But not completely!

Fact

King Tutankhamun was born about 1341 BC. He ruled from 1332 to 1323 BC. In AD, years are counted moving forward starting in year 1. But in BC, years are counted backward.

King Tut became pharaoh at just nine years old. He ruled Egypt for ten years.

In 1922, an amazing discovery rocked the world. Explorers discovered a nearly untouched tomb. They used science to investigate the tomb. Science revealed a fascinating story of early Egypt and the people who lived there. The story revolved around a very important person, King Tutankhamun. Today we know him as King Tut.

ANCIENT MARVELS

The most famous Egyptian tombs were built in the time known as the Old Kingdom from 2575 to 2130 BC. These tombs were the pyramids.

Pyramids were engineering marvels. Their sloped walls helped support each other. They didn't need support columns. This shape allowed the pyramids to have open spaces inside.

Workers mined limestone to build the pyramids. Their tools were made from stone or copper. Stronger metals such as iron and steel weren't common at that time. The Egyptians used sand to help the soft copper tools cut through the stone. The weight of the tools combined with the hardness of the sand quickly formed grooves in the limestone blocks.

Workers probably used ramps and rollers to lift the blocks. They used a mixture of sand and water to slide the heavy stones on the ramps. Wooden levers and bearings made of small, round stones were used to guide the blocks into place. Then workers shaped the blocks to fit them together perfectly.

Each stone block in a pyramid weighed about 2.5 tons.

Fact
The foundation of the Great Pyramid of Giza was level to within 0.8 inch (2 centimeters) and square to within 4.3 inches (11 cm).

DRY AS A BONE

During the time of the New Kingdom (1539–1075 BC), Egyptians wanted more private burials. They buried their royalty in the Valley of the Kings instead of in pyramids. This area of Egypt is very dry and hot. It's a great climate for preserving bodies and artifacts.

Every living organism has **bacteria** on it. When an organism dies, the bacteria begin breaking down its cells. This process is called decomposition. Even food and clothes made from plants or animals decompose. But bacteria need moisture to do their job. The Valley of the Kings is so dry that this process greatly slows down.

Entrances to tombs in the Valley of the Kings were well hidden among the rocky hills and cliffs.

The tombs in the Valley of the Kings were hidden deep in mountain shafts. However, many of these graves were discovered over time. Their treasures were often stolen. But archaeologists still hoped to find undiscovered tombs.

Ancient Egyptian Tombs and Temples

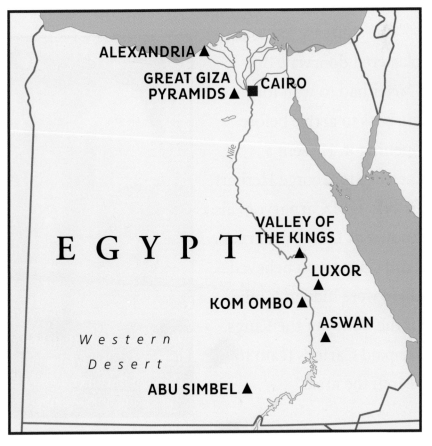

9

STUMBLING ONTO A SECRET

In 1917, British Egyptologist Howard Carter led an expedition to the Valley of the Kings. He hoped to find hidden tombs. He was unsuccessful for several years. Then on November 4, 1922, a member of Carter's crew stumbled upon a rock step. Digging furiously, Carter discovered a staircase. It led him to the greatest tomb discovery of our time.

The staircase led to a plastered doorway. But Carter had to wait for his boss to arrive before opening it. He sent a message to George Herbert, fifth Earl of Carnarvon, also known as Lord Carnarvon. Lord Carnarvon believed there were hidden tombs in the Valley of the Kings. He paid Carter's team to search the area.

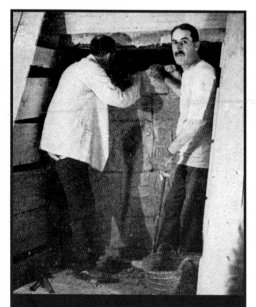

Lord Carnarvon (left) and Howard Carter (right) broke through the inner door of King Tut's tomb on November 26, 1922.

After Lord Carnarvon arrived, he and Carter opened the tomb door together. Inside was a passageway scattered with rubble and broken pottery. It had clearly been looted by thieves. But all hope wasn't lost. At the end of the passage was another door.

Carter chipped a small hole through the second door. He placed a candle inside the opening to test the air inside. Candles are used to test if mines or tunnels are safe to enter. Fire needs oxygen to burn. Humans need oxygen to breathe. If a flame goes out underground, it means there's not enough oxygen for people to breathe.

The Canary in the Coal Mine

Early coal miners used canaries to test mine safety. Canaries are very sensitive to toxic gases. Miners often took a caged canary with them into the mine. As long as the canary was alive and singing, they knew the mine was safe. If the canary suddenly died, the miners quickly left.

AN AMAZING DISCOVERY

As the warm air rushed out of the tomb, the candle flickered. But it didn't go out. Carter and Carnarvon carefully enlarged the hole to see inside. What they discovered shocked the world. They thought they'd find a one-room tomb. But instead they discovered four separate rooms.

The rooms had been carved into the limestone. About 100 years after the tomb was built, workmen digging the nearby tomb of King Ramses VI covered the rooms with a layer of rock chips. This accidental burial preserved much of the treasure.

The Layout of the Tomb

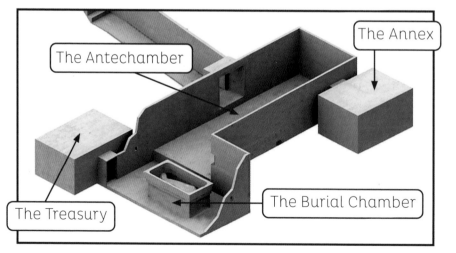

The Annex

The Antechamber

The Treasury

The Burial Chamber

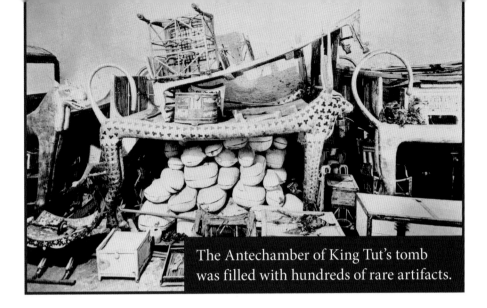
The Antechamber of King Tut's tomb was filled with hundreds of rare artifacts.

The tomb's doorways were topped with timber lintels. These beams supported the weight of the rock and rubble that was piled on top of the tomb. They spread the weight to the walls on either side of the doorway. The design of the lintels prevented the doorways from collapsing.

The rooms in the tomb were filled with rich treasures and artifacts. Inside the burial chamber was a large stone coffin called a sarcophagus. Carter believed it held the pharaoh's **mummified** body.

Fact

Scientists think there may be many undiscovered tombs in the Valley of the Kings. They are still looking for the tombs of several queens and the tomb of Ramses VIII.

CHAPTER 2

WHO WAS KING TUT?

Carter and his workers were eager to look inside the stone coffin. They actually found three coffins inside, stacked inside each other. The first two were gold-covered. The inner coffin was made of solid gold!

Ancient Egypt had many gold mines. The Egyptians prized gold in part because its color reminded them of Ra, the sun god. This metal was reserved for royalty, both alive and dead. Gold is malleable, meaning it can be hammered or pressed without breaking. Craftsmen hammered gold into a very thin layer to cover King Tut's two outer wooden coffins.

Fact

The Egyptians may have covered coffins with dark resin to honor Osiris. He was the god of the dead and the afterlife. Images of Osiris often showed him with black or dark green skin.

Howard Carter (left) used special solvents to remove and clean the resin that coated King Tut's inner coffin.

The inner, solid gold coffin was made from thicker sheets of gold that were pressed together. However, a dark, hard substance coated the inner coffin's lid. This substance contained resin, which is produced by plants such as pine trees. To get to the mummy, the coating had to be removed. Science came to the rescue.

Special liquid solvents were used to dissolve the resin. The substance and solvent must be similar for this to work. For example, salt and water are both **polar substances**. Water acts as a solvent when it dissolves salt. A solvent such as acetone dissolves resin. Heat can speed up the process.

PRESERVED IN TIME

King Tut's mummy was revealed nearly three years after the tomb was opened. He had been dead more than 3,000 years. But his body was still in good shape. The Egyptians believed people's souls were reunited with their bodies after death. But for the soul to find the body, it needed to be preserved.

The Egyptians understood the key to preserving bodies. They had to remove moisture that bacteria need to decompose cells. The first step was to cut small openings in the body to remove its organs. Hearts were mummified separately and returned to the body. Other organs were mummified and stored in containers called canopic jars.

Next, the Egyptians dried out the body. They covered it with a type of salt called natron. Salt removes water through osmosis. In this process, molecules move through cell walls. Water in cells moves out as salt moves in.

Lastly, they wrapped the body in layers of linen strips. They coated each layer with resin to hold the strips together. Mummifying a dead person made sure that the body would last for hundreds or thousands of years. Thanks to this process, modern people have learned much about King Tut.

coffin cover

linen strips

resin

canopic jars

The process to preserve a dead body as a mummy took about 70 days.

LIGHTING UP THE PAST

King Tut became king when he was just nine years old. Researchers knew he died at age 19. But the cause of his death was unknown. In 2005, scientists used a CT scan to study King Tut's body. A CT machine uses x-rays and a computer to form a cross-section image of the body. X-rays are invisible beams of light that pass through skin and body tissue. But they can't pass through dense things like bones. X-rays are captured on x-ray film or on a computer screen. Places where x-rays pass through look black. Thicker parts look white or gray. Doctors use x-rays to see a person's bones and body organs.

CT scans showed that King Tut had a cleft palate. This split in the roof of his mouth may have made eating and speaking difficult for him. His left foot also curved inward, which is known as a club foot.

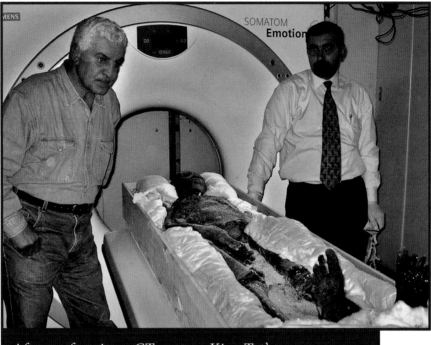

After performing a CT scan on King Tut's mummy, researchers learned that he suffered from a badly broken leg shortly before he died.

The scans also showed that King Tut had damaged ribs and a broken leg. Some researchers thought that he had been killed in a chariot wreck. Others thought he may have been attacked by a hippo while hunting. However, scientists later disproved these ideas.

Fact

More than 130 canes made of ivory, gold, and silver were in King Tut's tomb. Tut may have needed a cane to walk because of his club foot.

DECODING DNA

DNA analysis also provided a lot of information about King Tut. DNA, or deoxyribonucleic acid, is in every cell in an organism. DNA looks like a long, twisted chain. Each part of the chain contains different information. DNA copies itself when forming new cells. You may share traits such as hair or eye color with close relatives. You have copies of some parts of their DNA in your own cells.

Strands of DNA carry information that determines how an organism looks and functions.

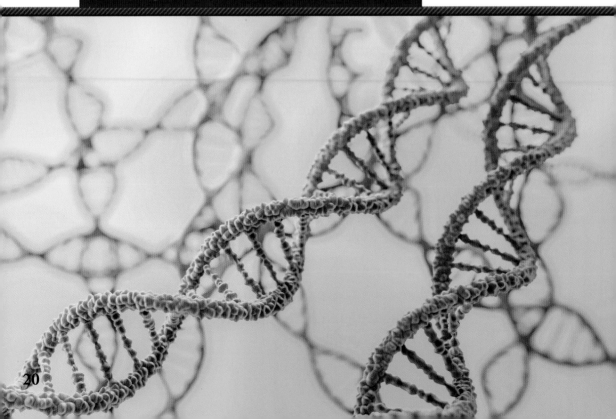

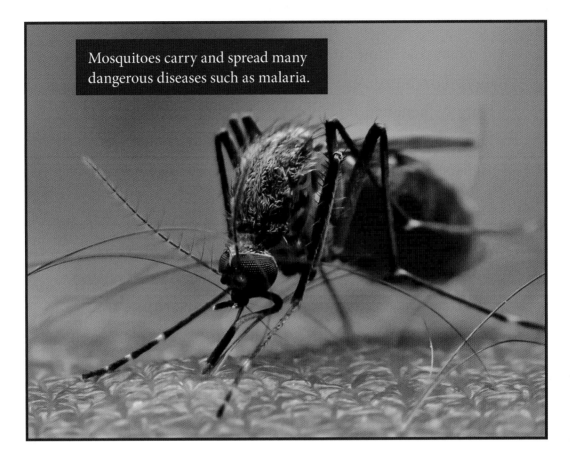

Mosquitoes carry and spread many dangerous diseases such as malaria.

Malaria is a disease caused by **parasites**. It is often passed to people through mosquito bites. Malaria has its own DNA. Malaria DNA was found in King Tut's body. Malaria can be deadly and may have played a part in his death.

TUT'S FAMILY TREE

Scientists compared King Tut's DNA to other known Egyptian mummies. They learned that his father was King Akhenaten. His mother's name is unknown, but DNA showed that Tut's parents likely were brother and sister.

It was common for royal Egyptian families to marry close relatives. This practice helped them keep power within the family. But it often had unhealthy effects on children. DNA contains genes. Genes determine traits such as eye color, height, and blood type. But genes can also carry illnesses. When close relatives have children together, it's more likely that genetic illnesses and defects will be passed on to them. King Tut's cleft palate and club foot may have been caused by these defects.

Tut and his sister-wife had two daughters who likely died at birth. The babies' mummies were also found in King Tut's tomb. They were in poorer condition than King Tut's mummy. But they appeared to have some genetic defects that may have caused their early deaths. These defects likely happened because Tut and his wife were related.

By studying King Tut's DNA, scientists learned that his wife, Ankhesenamun, was actually his half-sister.

SPECIAL SKULLS

Researchers noticed that King Tut had a unique head shape. The heads of many Egyptian pharaohs and queens had a similar oblong shape. Egyptian royals felt that their head shape set them apart from the common people.

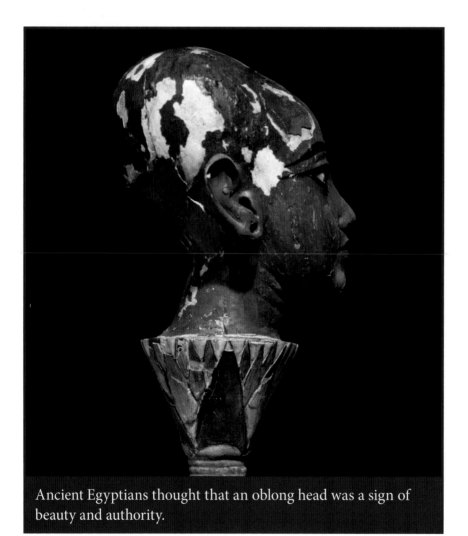

Ancient Egyptians thought that an oblong head was a sign of beauty and authority.

Royal Eyes

Images of King Tut's death mask show him wearing heavy black eye makeup. It was made from ground up minerals and was called kohl. It was common for wealthy Egyptian people to wear kohl. The dark eyeliner may have helped protect their eyes from the sun. It absorbed the sun's rays and shielded their eyes from glare.

King Tut as he may have looked while alive

Tut's head was likely shaped by head-binding. Many cultures through history have practiced head-binding. This practice works only on babies. Babies are born with six separate skull bones. The bones shift to allow a baby's head to fit through the birth canal. The separate bones also allow a baby's brain to grow. When the baby is between 12 and 18 months old, the bones fuse together, forming a solid skull. In ancient Egypt, royal parents bound their babies' heads with tight wraps. The wraps forced the bones to fuse together into an oblong shape.

CHAPTER 3

THE ARTIFACTS

Inside the layers of cloth around King Tut's mummy were several hidden treasures, including various jewels and weapons. But one of the finds puzzled researchers. Strapped to the mummy's thigh was a dagger. Its handle was made of gold, but its blade was iron. During King Tut's time, iron was much rarer than gold. Humans didn't commonly make iron objects until nearly 1,000 years after his death.

Howard Carter found two daggers within King Tut's wrappings. One was made with a golden blade. The other dagger's blade was made from rare iron.

Where did the iron come from? Scientists examined the blade with high-energy x-rays to learn what other metals were in it. The blade had a small amount of cobalt and was about 11 percent nickel. The amount was similar to what is found in meteorites. Scientists determined that King Tut's dagger had likely been hammered from a meteorite that fell from the sky. It was truly out of this world!

Shooting Stars

You've probably seen meteors. People often call these rocks shooting stars when they are seen in Earth's atmosphere. Most meteors are small and burn up before landing. If they hit Earth, they are called meteorites.

iron meteorite

HASTY BURIAL

The walls of King Tut's tomb also told a story. Usually tomb carvings instruct pharaohs on how to safely reach the afterlife. But Tut's tomb didn't contain these detailed carvings.

Instead the walls were covered with paintings. The paintings looked like they were done in a hurry. Drips in the paint were still visible. This shows that the tomb was prepared quickly, and that King Tut's death was probably sudden.

Some of the clothes and food packed inside Tut's tomb were crumbling. Some wooden objects also had broken down over time. But one thing that stayed in great shape was gold. Gold has unique properties. It is a basic element. Unlike other metals it doesn't corrode, or react with chemicals in the air. These reactions cause metal to rust or discolor. The golden objects in King Tut's tomb stayed bright and shiny.

The special properties of gold allowed King Tut's coffin to remain as bright and shiny as the day it was made.

Fact

Gold is often mixed with other metals to make it stronger. It's then used to make jewelry. The purity of gold is measured in karats. The purest gold is 24 karat.

CHARIOTS TO THE AFTERLIFE

Archaeologists saw that the tomb had been raided at least twice in the past. The doorways had been patched with different plaster at different times. Thieves had probably stolen some jewelry and smaller artifacts. But many weapons and other artifacts remained. These included swords, shields, boomerangs, clubs, and throw sticks. They were made from wood, leather, ivory, or bronze.

Along with the other treasures, six chariots were found inside Tut's tomb. Egyptian chariots were pulled by two horses. They were used for hunting and fighting. King Tut's chariots had some clever features. The wheel hubs were greased with animal fat. This **lubrication** helped reduce friction when the wheel turned on the axle. This in turn helped provide a smoother, faster ride. The chariots were also well balanced, with the axle near the back. This balance also helped to provide a smoother, more stable ride.

The Bronze Age

King Tut lived in the Bronze Age. This was a time in history when humans first began to use metal for tools instead of stone. Bronze is formed by combining melted tin and copper. Egyptians made bronze tools, weapons, doors, and jewelry.

Among the treasures in King Tut's tomb were several chariots. Some were covered with gold and jewels.

FROM SAND TO GLASS

King Tut's tomb also contained several containers and vases made from Egyptian **faience**. Faience is a composite material made from ground quartz with an **alkaline** glaze. Composite materials are made from two or more different materials. The materials don't change each other. They instead work together to make a stronger material.

The headrest in King Tut's coffin was made from blue faience.

Liquid or Solid?

Many people once believed that glass wasn't a solid substance. They thought it was a very slow-moving liquid. But scientists today know that glass is actually an amorphous solid. This means that the atoms and molecules in glass are arranged in random patterns. Most solids, such as crystal glass, have atoms and molecules arranged in a specific order.

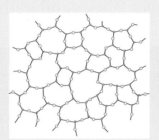

Atomic structure of amorphous glass

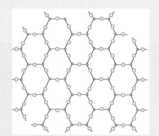

Atomic structure of crystal glass

Glass was also part of some of the objects in the tomb. The blue stripes on the headdress of Tut's death mask were made of glass. Egyptians were among the first people to make glass, beginning about 3500 BC. When sand is heated to 3,090 degrees Fahrenheit (1,700 degrees Celsius), it changes chemically. When it cools, it never goes back to its normal grittiness. It becomes the fragile, glossy material we know as glass.

KEPT IN THE DARK

Tombs protect artifacts from dangers in the natural environment. Danger awaits ancient artifacts when they are removed from a tomb. Ultraviolet (UV) light comes from the sun. We can't see this light, but it can cause a lot of damage. UV light causes sunburns on skin. It also damages fabrics and leather.

The dark, dry conditions in King Tut's tomb helped keep the artifacts inside in good shape. After removing the artifacts, researchers had to protect them from damaging moisture and sunlight.

The Electromagnetic Spectrum

Human eyes can see only a small part of the electromagnetic spectrum.

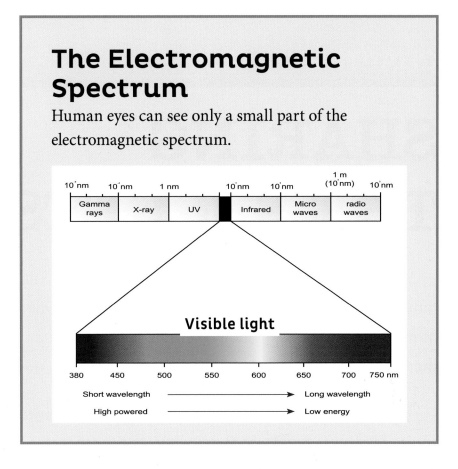

Moisture is another enemy. Moisture in the air is called humidity. Objects that have been stored in dry places absorb water when brought to a place with more humidity. The extra moisture can cause the objects to warp or swell.

Archaeologists try to protect artifacts by storing them in conditions similar to where they were found. This practice helps prevent the environment from destroying them.

CHAPTER 4

SHARING THE SECRETS

When people heard about the wonders in King Tut's tomb, they were anxious to see them. By the late 1980s, more than 4,000 people a day were taking tours of the tomb.

The tomb's wall paintings were covered with brown spots. The spots had been there when the tomb was opened. Scientists studying the tomb wondered what caused the brown spots and if they were increasing over time.

Fact

Millions of people have seen the treasures from King Tut's tomb. The artifacts were displayed around the world between 1972 and 1979.

Scientists used a high-powered microscope to look at the spots. They discovered that the spots were made of dead microbes. Microbes are very tiny organisms. The dead microbes were more evidence of King Tut's rushed burial. Microbes need moisture to live. The wall paint was likely still wet when the tomb was sealed. The moisture allowed the microbes to live for a time after the tomb was sealed. When the tomb dried out, the microbes died, leaving behind the brown spots.

Researchers learned that brown spots covering the walls of King Tut's tomb were created by ancient microbes.

SEARCH FOR NEFERTITI

Scientists found some surprises when they used lasers to scan the tomb. The scans showed shadows on the walls. Could these be hidden doors? The scientists hoped so. The doors could lead to the tomb of an important person. Queen Nefertiti was a well-known Egyptian queen. She is believed to have lived from about 1370 to 1330 BC.

Fact

Nefertiti is believed to have had an unusual amount of power for an Egyptian queen. She may even have ruled the country along with King Tut's father from about 1351 to 1334 BC. Archaeologists hope to find her tomb to learn more about her life.

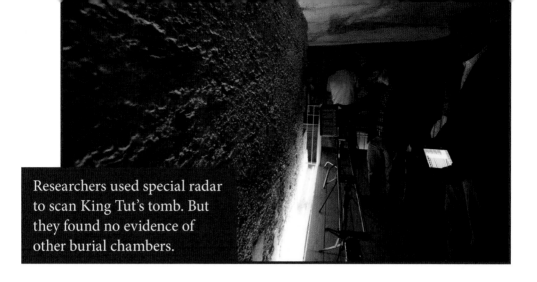

Researchers used special radar to scan King Tut's tomb. But they found no evidence of other burial chambers.

In 2015, scientists performed a ground-penetrating radar (GPR) scan of the area around King Tut's tomb. Radar works similar to light waves. Light waves bounce off objects before traveling to our eyes. This allows us to see the objects. Radar sends out radio waves, which also bounce back when they hit objects. A receiver listens for the waves. Radio waves bounce right back if they hit solid ground. But if there is an empty space behind a wall, the waves take longer to bounce back.

The first scan in 2015 was promising. It showed that hidden chambers were possible. Some researchers thought Nefertiti's tomb could be near King Tut's. However, a second scan in 2016 didn't show the same results. In 2018, three separate teams of scientists performed a scan and compared their results. Their investigation confirmed that Tut's tomb had no hidden chambers. Nefertiti's final resting place is still a mystery.

AN EXACT COPY

By the early 2000s, **carbon dioxide** and dust in the tomb were causing problems. Paint began to flake off the walls. Dust covered the precious wall paintings. In 2009, the tomb was closed to the public. It took nearly ten years to restore the wall paintings. Workers carefully cleaned off the dust, stabilized the flaking paint, and repaired any scratches or scrapes on the walls.

In the meantime, modern technology allowed people to keep "visiting" the tomb. In 2014, art technology company Factum Arte completed a full-sized, exact copy of the tomb. The company installed it near the house where Howard Carter once lived in Luxor, Egypt.

Laser scanning and 3D printing made the replica possible. A laser is a focused beam of light. When a scanner's laser moves over an object, it captures small details. The information is sent to a computer, which forms a 3D picture of the object. The images are then recreated by a 3D printer. These advanced printers push melted plastic through a nozzle. They lay down layer after layer of plastic **filament**, which slowly builds up a 3D shape.

An exact copy of King Tut's tomb was opened in 2014. Visitors can see the wonders of the tomb while keeping the real one safe.

3D printers lay down many layers of plastic or other material to create physical objects.

Fact

Experienced Egyptologists visited the replica of the tomb. Some had a hard time telling the difference between the replica and the actual tomb.

CHAPTER 5

THE CURSE OF KING TUT

When Carter and Lord Carnarvon opened King Tut's tomb, they found a statue of the god Anubis standing guard. Anubis was the Egyptian god of the underworld and the dead. The Anubis statue and ancient writings inside the tomb frightened some people. They believed that the tomb was cursed, and harm would come to people entering it.

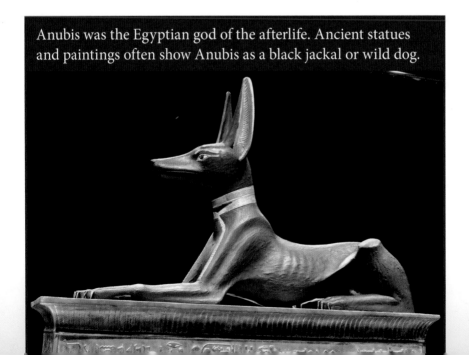

Anubis was the Egyptian god of the afterlife. Ancient statues and paintings often show Anubis as a black jackal or wild dog.

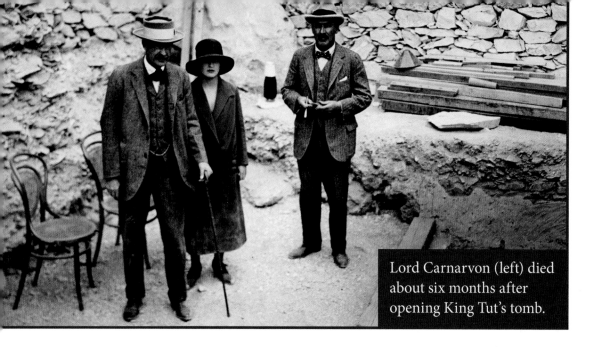

Lord Carnarvon (left) died about six months after opening King Tut's tomb.

Lord Carnarvon later died on April 5, 1923. Some people believed that the curse had killed him. However, he actually died from blood poisoning that was caused by a mosquito bite. Another name for blood poisoning is **sepsis**. This condition happens when bacteria enters a person's bloodstream. Sepsis can cause damage to the body's organs and lead to death.

Many people at the time believed in King Tut's curse. But no scientific evidence supports that idea. At least 58 people were present in the tomb when Tut's coffin was opened. Eight years later, 50 of them were still alive. Carter was one of them. He lived until 1939 when he died of cancer.

MICROSCOPIC DANGER

King Tut's curse wasn't real. But something dangerous does lurk in Egypt's dark tombs. A number of workers have become sick after being inside tombs. Doctors investigated and found that some workers were exposed to black mold.

Laboratory tests show that some mummies contain dangerous kinds of mold. Molds are **fungi**. This group of organisms are neither plants nor animals. But they are important helpers in decomposition. When fungi are disturbed, they release spores into the air. Some kinds of spores can be poisonous. When people breathe in these spores, they can become sick.

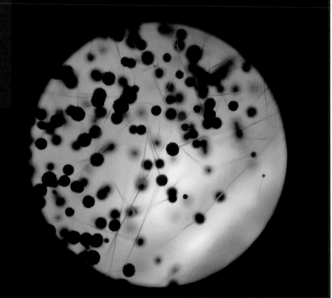

Spores from certain kinds of mold can be poisonous. They can cause serious health problems for people.

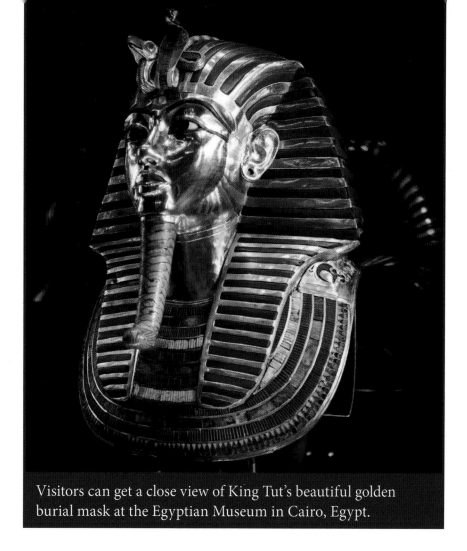

Visitors can get a close view of King Tut's beautiful golden burial mask at the Egyptian Museum in Cairo, Egypt.

Are fungi an ancient curse? It's doubtful. They are just one of the many fascinating features related to the tombs of Ancient Egypt. King Tut's tomb was one of the greatest discoveries ever made. Science has helped the world get to know the young pharaoh and his life. Science will likely continue to shed light on the lives of people who lived thousands of years ago.

GLOSSARY

alkaline (AL-kuh-luhn)—a substance that measures greater than 7 on the pH scale; alkaline solutions are considered basic rather than acidic

bacteria (bak-TEER-ee-uh)—one-celled, microscopic living things that exist all around you and inside you; many bacteria are useful, but some cause disease

carbon dioxide (KAHR-buhn dy-AHK-syd)—a colorless, odorless gas that people and animals breathe out

faience (FAY-ants)—a type of clay pottery decorated with colored glazes

filament (FI-luh-muhnt)—a thin fiber

fungi (FUHN-jy)—organisms that have no leaves, flowers, or roots; mushrooms and molds are fungi

lubrication (loo-bruh-KAY-shuhn)—the process of applying a substance that reduces friction and wear between two surfaces

mummify (MUH-mi-fye)—to preserve a dead body with special salts and cloth; a mummified body is called a mummy

parasite (PAIR-uh-site)—an organism that lives on or in another organism to get food or protection

polar substance (POH-luhr SUHB-stuhnss)—a substance that mixes easily with water; polar substances contain both positive and negative charges

sepsis (SEP-suhs)—a toxic illness caused by bacteria; sepsis is also called blood poisoning

READ MORE

Drimmer, Stephanie Warren. *Ancient Egypt*. Washington, DC: National Geographic Kids, 2018.

Loh-Hagan, Virginia. *The Real King Tut*. Ann Arbor, MI: Cherry Lake Press, 2019.

Oachs, Emily Rose. *King Tut's Tomb*. Minneapolis: Bellwether Media, 2020.

Peterson, Megan Cooley. *King Tut: Is His Tomb Really Cursed?* Mankato, MN: Black Rabbit Books, 2019.

INTERNET SITES

Biography: King Tut
www.biography.com/royalty/king-tut

King Tut for Kids
www.ancient-egypt-online.com/king-tut-for-kids.html

Mummy Mystery: King Tut
kids.nationalgeographic.com/explore/history/king-tut/

INDEX